BOYS AND GIRLS
COOKBOOK

Ideals Publishing Corporation
Nashville, Tennessee

CONTENTS

This book is one of a series of cookbooks including the following titles:

Budget Saving Meals Cookbook
Chicken and Poultry Cookbook
Grill and Barbecue Cooking
Ground Meat Cookbook
Guide to Microwave Cookbook
Hershey's Chocolate and Cocoa Cookbook
Low Calorie Cookbook
Lunch and Brunch Cookbook
Old-Fashioned Family Cookbook
Soup, Salad and Sandwich Cookbook
Quick & Simple Cooking for Two

30-Minute Meals Cookbook
All Holidays Menus Cookbook
American Regional Cookbook
Boys & Girls Cookbook
Christmas Cookbook
Country Baking Cookbook
Fish and Seafood Cookbook
Light & Delicious Cookbook
Casseroles & One Dish Meals
New Salad Cookbook
Wok Cookbook

These and other Ideals books are available in a SOFTCOVER edition in bulk quantities at quantity discount for fund-raising or premium use. For information, please write SPECIAL SALES DEPARTMENT, Ideals Publishing Corporation, P.O. Box 140300, Nashville, TN 37214

The HARDCOVER edition of selected Titles is published in a limited edition for the exclusive use of Wayne Matthews Corporation, P.O. Box 54, Safety Harbor, FL 34695.

ISBN 0-8249-3079-7

Published by Ideals Publishing Corporation
Nelson Place at Elm Hill Pike
Nashville, Tennessee 37214-8000

Cover Photo:
Mexican Munch Olé, 49;
Nutty Haystacks, 58;
Granola, 56;
Pop-a-Pizza, 63

Zebra Parfaits, 40;
Smart Snacks with Wonder Dip, 32;
Pizza Planks, 61;

Before You Start

Always get permission before you cook and make sure an adult is nearby in case you run into a problem or need some assistance.

Read the recipe before you start, and make sure you have all the ingredients on hand.

Wear an apron, tie back your hair if it is long, and wash your hands.

Get out the equipment listed in the recipe.

Measure the ingredients listed in the recipe.

Ask an adult to help you when cutting or chopping. Always cut down, with the knife blade toward the cutting board, and keep your fingers out of the way.

Keep your work area tidy. Put food away as soon as you are done with it, especially those needing refrigeration. Clean up spills immediately so no one slips and falls.

Don't forget to clean up after you cook. Put everything away and leave a tidy kitchen.

Cooking Safety

Before you use a sharp knife, can opener, broiler, blender, mixer, or microwave oven, be sure an adult is in the kitchen to help you.

Ask an adult to drain large amounts of food cooked in hot water. If it isn't done correctly, the steam could burn you.

Turn the handles of pans on the range away from you so they won't catch on something and tip over. Also be sure they are not over another burner.

Dry your hands after washing them to avoid slippery fingers or electrical shocks.

Clean up all spills immediately.

Always turn the sharp edge of a knife or paring instrument away from you and keep fingers out of the way.

Use thick, dry pot holders. Thin or wet pads do not provide adequate protection from the heat.

Turn off blender or mixer before scraping the side of the container so that rubber spatula or spoon won't get caught in blades.

Turn off and unplug mixer before putting beaters in or taking them out.

Never disconnect an appliance by pulling on the cord; pull the plug out of the socket.

Be sure to turn off oven or range when you are finished cooking.

Using Your Appliances
The Oven

Move shelves to the correct position before turning the oven on.

Allow plenty of air space around each item you are baking—containers should not touch each other.

Alternate position of foods on each shelf so that one is not directly over another.

Use a tight-fitting cover or aluminum foil when a recipe calls for covering the pan.

Close the oven door quickly so that heat will not escape.

The Range

Place large pans on large burners and small pans on small burners. Turn the pan handles so they do not hang out over the edge of the range, and also make sure they are not over another burner.

The Microwave Oven

Read the instruction booklet to find out which types of food your oven can handle and the correct cooking times.

Cover foods as instructed to prevent spattering.

Allow foods to stand for a few minutes after removal from the oven as they keep on cooking when you take them out.

Be careful not to burn yourself. Microwaves go through containers without making them hot, but the food in the container may make it hot.

Measuring Equivalents

3 teaspoons = 1 tablespoon
½ tablespoon = 1½ teaspoons
4 tablespoons = ¼ cup
5 tablespoons
   + 1 teaspoon = ⅓ cup
16 tablespoons = 1 cup
2 cups = 1 pint
4 cups = 2 pints = 1 quart
4 quarts = 1 gallon

Butter or Margarine

½ stick = ⅛ pound = ¼ cup
1 stick = ¼ pound = ½ cup
4 sticks = 1 pound = 2 cups

Measuring Equipment and Methods

Dry measure cups are for measuring dry ingredients such as flour, sugar, brown sugar, cornstarch, and other dry ingredients. For most ingredients, just fill the measuring cup and level off with a spatula. Brown sugar is measured differently; it is packed firmly, and then leveled off. Shortening is also packed before leveling off.

Glass measures are used for measuring liquids. They have spouts for pouring liquids without spilling. To measure accurately, bend down so your eyes are level with the measurement mark you need. Slowly pour in the liquid; stop when it reaches the correct mark.

Measuring spoons are used for measuring small amounts, either dry or liquid. Fill the spoon with the ingredient and if dry, level off with a spatula.

Butter and margarine are very easy to measure; 1 stick is equal to ½ cup. Most wrappers are marked in tablespoons. All you need to do is cut through the wrapper and butter at the correct measurement line.

BREAKFAST BEGINNINGS

Crisp Bacon Slices

INGREDIENTS:

4 slices bacon

EQUIPMENT:

Paper towels
12 x 8-inch glass baking
  dish
Plate
Fork

1. Place 2 layers of paper towels in the glass dish.

2. Place bacon slices on top.

3. Cover bacon with another paper towel.

4. Microwave bacon on HIGH for 2 minutes 45 seconds to 3½ minutes, until golden and crisp.

5. Carefully remove the dish from microwave. Push the top towel back with a fork.

6. Line a plate with a clean paper towel. With a fork, carefully transfer cooked bacon to the towel-lined plate. This will absorb any excess grease.

Bacon Popovers

Makes 6 servings

INGREDIENTS:

10 slices bacon
 2 eggs
 1 cup milk
 1 cup flour
   Honey *or* butter

EQUIPMENT:

Knife
Large skillet
Paper towels
Medium-sized bowl
Fork
6 6-ounce, well-greased
  custard cups
Cookie sheet

1. Preheat oven to 450°.

2. Use knife to cut bacon into ½-inch pieces.

3. Cook in large skillet on medium-low heat until crisp.

4. Drain bacon on a paper towel.

5. Combine eggs, milk, and flour in medium-sized bowl. Beat with fork until smooth.

6. Stir in bacon pieces.

7. Pour mixture into custard cups.

8. Place cups on cookie sheet and bake in 450° oven for 20 minutes.

9. Decrease temperature to 350° and bake 15 more minutes.

10. Serve with honey or butter.

Banana Wrap

Makes 1 serving

INGREDIENTS:

- 1 8-inch flour tortilla
- 2 to 3 tablespoons peanut butter
- 2 to 3 tablespoons grape jelly
- 1 small banana, peeled

EQUIPMENT:

Measuring spoons
Paper towel
Table knife

1. Place tortilla on a paper towel. Microwave 10 to 20 seconds on HIGH until the tortilla is soft and warm.

2. Spread with peanut butter.

3. Top with grape jelly.

4. Place the banana near the right edge of the tortilla.

5. Fold up the bottom fourth of the tortilla.

6. Bring right edge over the banana and roll up.

Breakfast Cookies

Makes 2½ dozen

INGREDIENTS:

- 10 slices bacon
- ½ cup butter *or* margarine, softened
- 1 egg
- 2 tablespoons frozen orange juice concentrate
- ¼ cup sugar
- 1 cup flour
- 1 teaspoon baking powder
- 2 cups corn flakes
- ¼ cup wheat germ

EQUIPMENT:

Skillet
Paper towels
Large bowl
Measuring cups and spoons
Large spoon
Cookie sheet
Fork

1. Preheat oven to 350°.

2. Cook bacon in skillet on medium-low heat until crisp. Drain on a paper towel, then crumble into large bowl.

3. Add next four ingredients; blend well with spoon.

4. Stir in remaining ingredients.

5. Shape into 1-inch balls.

6. Place on ungreased cookie sheet.

7. Flatten with fork dipped in flour.

8. Bake in oven 12 to 15 minutes until golden brown.

9. Wrap and store in refrigerator.

Fruit Kabobs

Makes 1 serving

INGREDIENTS:

- 3 banana slices (½-inch thick)
- 3 strawberries
- 3 grapes
- 1 pineapple chunk
- 1 maraschino cherry

EQUIPMENT:

One 6-inch wooden skewer

1. Stick the banana slices, strawberries, and grapes, in any order, on the wooden skewer.

2. Decorate the end of the skewer with a pineapple chunk and maraschino cherry.

Hash Brown Omelet

Makes 4 servings

INGREDIENTS:

- 4 slices bacon
- 3 cups cooked packaged hash browns
- ¼ cup chopped onion
- ¼ cup chopped green pepper
- ¾ teaspoon salt
- 4 beaten eggs
- ¼ cup milk
- ¼ teaspoon dried thyme, crushed
  Pepper
- 1 cup shredded Swiss cheese

EQUIPMENT:

Measuring cups and spoons
Knife
Large bowl
Large skillet with lid
Spoon
Spatula

1. In skillet, cook bacon until crisp; remove from skillet and leave about 2 tablespoons of drippings in pan.

2. Crumble bacon into bowl.

3. Combine potatoes, onion, green pepper, and ½ teaspoon of the salt in skillet. Cook over low heat for about 20 minutes until underside is crispy.

4. To the bowl with the bacon, add eggs, milk, thyme, the remaining ¼ teaspoon salt, and dash pepper. Stir in cheese; pour over potatoes.

5. Cover; cook over low heat 8 to 10 minutes or until surface is set but still shiny.

6. Loosen edges of omelet and cut into wedges to serve.

Egg Ragamuffin

Makes 1 serving

INGREDIENTS:

- 1 teaspoon butter
- 1 egg
- 1 teaspoon water
- 1 English muffin, split and toasted
- 1 thin slice cooked ham
  Salt and pepper
- 1 teaspoon mustard

EQUIPMENT:

Measuring spoons
Small skillet
Small bowl
Fork

1. Melt butter in small skillet over low heat. Swirl butter around to grease the sides of skillet.

2. Place ham in skillet. Cook over low heat for 15 to 20 seconds on each side. Remove ham from pan.

3. Blend egg and water with a fork in a small bowl. Pour into same pan in which ham was cooked.

4. Cook over medium heat about 3 minutes, stirring occasionally with a fork.

5. Fold ham slice to fit onto bottom half of English muffin. Slide egg out and onto ham. Salt and pepper to taste.

6. Spread mustard on top half of muffin and place it over egg.

French Toast

Makes 6 servings

INGREDIENTS:

- 2 eggs
- ½ cup milk
- ¼ teaspoon vanilla extract
- 6 slices white bread (day-old bread is easier to work with than fresh bread)
  Powdered sugar *or* pancake syrup

EQUIPMENT:

Large skillet
Small bowl
Fork
Spatula

1. Beat together eggs, milk, and vanilla in a small bowl; set aside.

2. Melt butter in a large skillet over medium heat.

3. Dip bread, one slice at a time, into egg mixture.

4. Cook bread 2 or 3 pieces at a time in the skillet (do not overcrowd skillet as the bread will not brown evenly). Cook about 3 to 4 minutes on each side or until brown. Turn with spatula and remove from pan with spatula.

5. Serve with powdered sugar or pancake syrup.

Egg Ragamuffin, this page;
Fruit Kabobs, 9

Egg in a Hole

Makes 1 serving

INGREDIENTS:

1½ tablespoons butter *or* margarine
1 slice bread
1 egg
  Salt and pepper

EQUIPMENT:

Round cookie cutter
Table knife
Small skillet
Spatula

1. Cut center out of slice of bread with a round cookie cutter or glass. Butter both sides of remaining bread, using about ½ tablespoon butter.

2. Melt remaining tablespoon butter in a small skillet over medium heat. Brown one side of bread in skillet; turn bread over.

3. Break egg into a small cup or saucer. Carefully slip it into the hole in the bread slice in the skillet. Sprinkle salt and pepper on egg.

4. Cook egg until white is set. Use spatula to remove from skillet.

Note: If desired, turn bread and egg to brown both sides of egg.

Breakfast Bars

Makes 8 servings

INGREDIENTS:

¾ cup quick-cooking oatmeal
¼ cup applesauce
4 canned apricots, chopped; reserve ¼ cup juice in small cup
1 cup raisins
½ cup powdered milk
2 tablespoons cocoa
2 tablespoons brown sugar
1 tablespoon sesame seeds
¾ teaspoon coconut extract
¼ teaspoon salt
1 tablespoon butter *or* margarine

EQUIPMENT:

Small cup
Measuring cups and spoons
Medium-sized mixing bowl
8 x 8-inch baking pan

1. Preheat oven to 350°.

2. In mixing bowl, mix first 10 ingredients. Add apricot juice and blend well.

3. Use the butter to grease the 8 x 8-inch pan.

4. Spread the mixture in the pan.

5. Bake for 15 minutes, or until the mixture is not sticky to touch.

6. Cut into strips while warm.

Muffin Surprise

Makes 1½ dozen

INGREDIENTS:

- 1 egg
- 1 cup milk
- ¼ cup vegetable oil
- 2 cups all-purpose flour
- ¼ cup sugar
- 1 tablespoon baking powder
- 1 teaspoon salt
- 3 tablespoons jelly *or* jam

EQUIPMENT:

Muffin pans
Paper baking cups, optional
Medium-sized mixing bowl
Fork
Small bowl
Large spoon
Teaspoon
Table knife

1. Preheat oven to 400°. Grease the bottoms of muffin cups or line with paper baking cups.

2. Beat egg, milk, and oil together in medium-sized bowl.

3. Mix flour, sugar, baking powder, and salt together in small bowl. Add all at once to the egg mixture. Stir just until flour is moistened.

4. Fill each muffin cup ⅓ full with batter. Drop about ½ teaspoon jelly or jam into the center of each cup and top with enough batter to fill cups ⅔ full. Wipe off any spilled batter before placing pans in oven.

5. Place pan in oven and bake for 20 to 25 minutes or until golden brown. Loosen the sides of muffins with table knife and remove from pan immediately.

Mexican Breakfast

Makes 1 serving

INGREDIENTS:

- 2 slices cooked ham
- 1 flour tortilla, 7-inch diameter
- 1 tablespoon butter *or* margarine
- 1 beaten egg
- 2 tablespoons shredded Cheddar cheese
- 1 tablespoon chopped onion
- Chili powder

EQUIPMENT:

Measuring spoons
Small skillet with lid
Spatula

1. Overlap ham on tortilla.

2. Melt butter in skillet.

3. Place tortilla with meat in skillet.

4. Top with egg, cheese, and onion.

5. Cover skillet with lid and cook over medium-low heat 5 minutes or until egg is set.

6. Sprinkle with chili powder and fold in half to eat.

Wild West Chili

Makes 6 servings

INGREDIENTS:

1 pound lean ground beef
1 package (1¼ ounces) chili seasoning
1 can (10¾ ounces) tomato soup
⅓ cup water
1 can (15 ounces) chili beans

EQUIPMENT:

Measuring cup
Large skillet
Wooden spoon

1. Place ground beef in skillet. Cook over medium-low heat for 5 to 7 minutes, until meat is no longer pink. Stir meat occasionally during cooking with a wooden spoon so that it will brown evenly.

2. Add chili seasoning; stir with a wooden spoon to mix.

3. Add tomato soup, water, and chili beans. Stir to combine the ingredients.

4. Continue cooking for 15 to 20 minutes, or until chili begins to boil.

5. Reduce heat to low, and simmer for 15 to 20 minutes.

Fiesta Burgers

Makes 2 servings

INGREDIENTS:

½ pound lean ground beef
1 tablespoon taco seasoning mix
2 tablespoons mild taco sauce
2 hamburger buns, toasted
Shredded cheese
Shredded lettuce
Chopped tomato
Avocado dip
Taco sauce

EQUIPMENT:

Small mixing bowl
Measuring spoons
Fork
Medium-sized skillet
Wide spatula

1. In a small mixing bowl, combine the ground beef, taco seasoning mix, and taco sauce. Mix well with a fork.

2. Shape into two patties.

3. Heat skillet over medium heat 1 minute.

4. Arrange patties in skillet. Cook 5 minutes on each side. Use spatula to turn burgers to prevent burning.

5. Remove burgers from skillet with spatula. Place on buns.

6. Top each Fiesta Burger with cheese, lettuce, and tomato. Serve with avocado dip and taco sauce.

Onion Burgers

Makes 6 servings

INGREDIENTS:

1 baking potato
1 pound ground beef
1 tablespoon instant
   minced onion
1 tablespoon catsup
1 teaspoon salt
   Dash ground black
    pepper
6 hamburger buns

EQUIPMENT:

Measuring spoons
Vegetable peeler
Vegetable grater
Large mixing bowl
10-inch skillet
Metal spatula

1. Peel potato with vegetable peeler and shred into mixing bowl with grater.

2. Mix in ground beef, onion, catsup, salt, and pepper.

3. Shape mixture into 6 patties.

4. Heat skillet over medium heat 1 minute.

5. Arrange patties in skillet. Cook 5 minutes on each side. Use spatula to turn burgers and to remove from skillet.

6. Serve on buns.

Foil Dinner

Makes 4 servings

INGREDIENTS:

3 carrots
3 stalks celery
1 small onion
2 medium potatoes
4 chicken breasts *or* thighs
   Butter *or* margarine
   Salt and pepper

EQUIPMENT:

Knife
Paper towels
Heavy-duty aluminum foil

1. Preheat oven to 350°.

2. Cut carrots, celery, onion, and potatoes into bite-sized pieces.

3. Wash chicken under cold water; pat dry with a paper towel.

4. Place one piece of chicken and ¼ of the vegetables on each of four pieces of aluminum foil.

5. Add a pat of butter to each and season with salt and pepper.

6. Bring foil up over chicken and fold edges tightly.

7. Bake for 1 hour or until chicken and potatoes are tender.

Italian Squiggles

Makes 6 servings

INGREDIENTS:

1 pound lean ground beef
1 jar (15½ ounces) Italian
    spaghetti sauce
2½ cups water
8 ounces corkscrew-
    shaped pasta
    Parmesan cheese,
    grated, optional

EQUIPMENT:

Plastic colander
2-quart microwave-safe
    batter bowl
Paper towels
Wooden spoon
Measuring cups
Waxed paper
Potholders

1. Place ground beef in large skillet. Cook over medium-low heat for 5 to 7 minutes until meat is no longer pink. Stir meat occasionally during cooking with a wooden spoon so that it will brown evenly.

2. Remove skillet from heat. Have an adult help you drain excess grease from pan with a spoon.

3. Return pan to heat; add spaghetti sauce and water. Cook over medium heat until mixture comes to a boil.

4. Add the pasta. Reduce heat and simmer, uncovered, for 10 to 15 minutes, until pasta is tender. Stir with wooden spoon occasionally to prevent pasta from sticking to pan bottom.

5. Remove from heat. Sprinkle with cheese and serve immediately.

Tuna Macaroni Salad

Makes 6 servings

INGREDIENTS:

1 cup elbow *or* shell
    macaroni
¾ cup mayonnaise
1 tablespoon lemon juice
1 7-ounce can tuna,
    drained and flaked
1 green onion, chopped
1 teaspoon salt

EQUIPMENT:

Measuring cups and spoons
Saucepan
Fork
Large mixing bowl

1. Cook macaroni in saucepan according to directions.

2. Combine all ingredients in bowl and toss gently to mix well.

3. Cover and refrigerate for 1 hour.

Tomato Squash

Makes 2 servings

INGREDIENTS:

1 **large acorn squash**
¼ **pound ground beef**
2 **tablespoons tomato paste**
½ **teaspoon salt**
¼ **teaspoon pepper**
1 **small tomato, peeled and sliced**
1 **tablespoon diced green pepper**

EQUIPMENT:

Measuring spoons
Knife
Spoon
Bowl
Fork

1. Preheat oven to 375°.
2. If squash will not stand, use knife to slice a small piece off the bottom to level it out.
3. Cut the top off the squash in a straight line and keep the top. Scrape out seeds and discard.
4. Mix ground beef with all other ingredients in bowl and fill squash with the mixture.
5. Put on the squash top.
6. Bake 45 minutes to 1 ¼ hours depending on size of squash. Fork will easily pierce squash when fully cooked.
7. Cut in half to serve.

Zesty Drumsticks

Makes 3 to 4 servings

INGREDIENTS:

3 **tablespoons butter *or* margarine**
¾ **cup cornflake crumbs**
¼ **cup grated Parmesan cheese**
½ **teaspoon Italian herb seasoning**
¾ **teaspoon seasoned salt**
6 **chicken drumsticks, about 1¼ pounds**

EQUIPMENT:

Measuring cups and spoons
Small saucepan
Large plastic food bag
9 x 13-inch baking dish
Potholders

1. Preheat oven to 425°.
2. Melt butter in a small saucepan over low heat and set aside.
3. Combine crumbs, cheese, herb seasoning, and salt in a food bag. Twist top and shake the bag to mix the ingredients.
4. Wash chicken pieces and pat them dry. Drop chicken, 3 pieces at a time, into the bag of crumbs. Shake bag to coat chicken.
5. Arrange chicken pieces in a single layer in baking dish.
6. Drizzle the melted butter over the chicken.
7. Bake, uncovered, 45 minutes, or until chicken is tender.

Grilled Ham and Cheese

Makes 2 servings

INGREDIENTS:

4 slices bread
2 slices American cheese
2 thin slices cooked ham
2 tablespoons butter *or* margarine

EQUIPMENT:

Skillet
Cookie sheet

1. Preheat oven to 300°.
2. Place a slice of cheese and a slice of ham on 2 pieces of bread.
3. Cover with remaining bread and press firmly together.
4. Melt butter in skillet over low heat.
5. Dip both sides of each sandwich in the butter.
6. Lay sandwiches on a cookie sheet and bake 5 to 10 minutes or until cheese melts.
7. Cut diagonally and serve hot.

Hot Chicken Salad

Makes 4 to 6 servings

INGREDIENTS:

3 cups cooked chicken *or* turkey chunks
2 hard-boiled eggs, diced, optional
1 10½-ounce can cream of chicken soup
1 teaspoon instant minced onion
¾ cup mayonnaise
1 tablespoon lemon juice
2 large stalks celery
2 strips green pepper
1 tablespoon butter *or* margarine
15 potato chips

EQUIPMENT:

Measuring cups and spoons
Large mixing bowl
Kitchen scissors
Mixing spoon
1½-quart casserole
Plastic bag
Rolling pin

1. Preheat oven to 350°.
2. Put chicken, eggs, soup, onion, mayonnaise, and lemon juice in bowl.
3. Cut celery and pepper into small pieces with scissors. Add to bowl.
4. Stir with mixing spoon.
5. Grease casserole with butter. Pour chicken mixture into casserole.
6. Crush potato chips in plastic bag by rolling with rolling pin.
7. Sprinkle over chicken mixture.
8. Bake 30 to 40 minutes. Serve immediately.

Easy Beef Stew

Makes 6 to 8 servings

INGREDIENTS:

3 to 4 tablespoons flour
½ teaspoon crushed oregano
  Salt and pepper
2 pounds beef round steak
  or stew meat
2 to 3 tablespoons butter
  or margarine
6 medium carrots
6 medium potatoes
1 small onion
1 can (10¼ ounces) tomato soup
1 can (10¼ ounces) beef consommé

EQUIPMENT:

Plastic food bag
Cutting board
Sharp knife
Medium-sized skillet
Wooden spoon
Vegetable parer
Large (3- to 4-quart) casserole dish with lid (use aluminum foil if lid is not available)
Fork
Small mixing bowl
Large spoon

1. Preheat oven to 325°.

2. Place flour, oregano, and salt and pepper in plastic food bag. Twist top and shake to mix.

3. Cut stew meat into 1-inch cubes on cutting board. Toss beef cubes in bag with flour mixture.

4. Melt butter in medium-sized skillet over medium-low heat. Add meat to skillet and cook for 5 to 8 minutes. Stir with a wooden spoon occasionally so that meat browns evenly.

5. Remove skillet from heat and transfer meat to casserole dish.

6. Wash and pare carrots and potatoes; peel onion. Cut each of carrots into 2-inch pieces; cut potatoes into quarters. Chop onion into small pieces.

7. Mix vegetables and meat in casserole dish with a fork.

8. Stir together tomato soup and consommé in a small bowl. Pour over vegetables and meat; mix well with a large spoon.

9. Place casserole dish in oven and cover with lid or with aluminum foil. (If using foil, cover tightly.)

10. Bake for 2 to 2½ hours, or until vegetables are tender when pierced with a fork.

Frankfurter Casserole

Makes 6 servings

INGREDIENTS:

- 4 slices bacon
- 1 10¾-ounce can condensed cream of mushroom soup
- 1 tablespoon instant minced onion
- ½ teaspoon salt
- 1 8-ounce can peas, drained
- 1 16-ounce can whole kernel corn, drained
- 1 15-ounce can sliced potatoes, drained
- 6 frankfurters, sliced crosswise

EQUIPMENT:

2-quart casserole
Potholders
Rubber spatula
Measuring spoons
Small frying pan
Tongs
Paper towels
Cutting board
Knife

1. Preheat oven to 350°.

2. Carefully use a knife to slice bacon and frankfurters into ½-inch pieces.

3. Place bacon pieces in small frying pan. Fry over medium heat until crisp.

4. Remove bacon and place on paper towels to drain. Set aside. Place soup, onion, and salt in 2-quart casserole. Stir in peas, corn, potatoes, and sliced frankfurters.

5. Sprinkle bacon over the top.

6. Place in oven and bake for 45 minutes. Carefully remove from oven with potholders.

Wild West Chili, 15

Turkey French Toast

Makes 6 servings

INGREDIENTS:

- 1 cup minced turkey
- 1 tablespoon sweet pickle relish
- ¼ cup chopped celery
- ¼ cup mayonnaise
- 12 slices bread
- 3 eggs, slightly beaten
- ¾ cup milk
- 1 teaspoon sugar
- 1 tablespoon butter *or* margarine

EQUIPMENT:

Measuring cups and spoons
2 bowls
Knife
Fork
Hot griddle *or* skillet

1. Mince turkey by carefully cutting into very small pieces with a knife.

2. Combine turkey, relish, celery, and mayonnaise in a bowl. Mix well.

3. Spread mixture on 6 slices of bread.

4. Top with other 6 slices of bread.

5. Beat eggs, milk, and sugar together in other bowl.

6. Dip sandwiches in egg mixture and fry in table-spoon of butter on hot griddle or skillet until golden.

7. Cut diagonally and serve hot.

Mock Turtle Soup

Makes 3 to 4 servings

INGREDIENTS:

- 2 medium potatoes
- 3 stalks celery
- 1 small onion
- 2 carrots
  Salt to taste
- 2 cups water
- 2 tablespoons Cheez Whiz *or* melted Cheddar cheese
- 3 cups milk

EQUIPMENT:

Measuring cups and spoons
Knife
Saucepan

1. Wash vegetables and use knife to cut into bite-sized pieces.

2. Place in saucepan with water and simmer for 35 minutes or until tender.

3. Next, add cheese and stir well.

4. Add milk and a little more water if soup is too thick. Heat on low setting until warm and serve.

Cheesy Bacon Shells

Makes 6 servings

INGREDIENTS:

- 1 small package bacon
- 1 10- to 12-ounce package jumbo shell macaroni
- 1 10-ounce package frozen chopped spinach, thawed
- 1 8-ounce package cream cheese
- 1 egg

Sauce:

- 1 small onion, chopped
- 1 16-ounce can stewed tomatoes
- 1 8-ounce can tomato sauce

EQUIPMENT:

Knife
Skillet
Paper towels
Measuring spoons
Small bowl
Saucepan
Colander
Mixing bowl
2-quart casserole with lid

1. Preheat oven to 350°.

2. Cut bacon into ½-inch pieces and cook in skillet on medium-low heat until crisp.

3. Remove bacon and place on paper towel. Reserve 1 tablespoon drippings and discard the rest.

4. Cook shells in saucepan according to directions on package. Rinse under cold water.

5. Place spinach in colander; press to remove excess water.

6. Combine spinach, cream cheese, egg, and half of bacon pieces in bowl.

7. Fill each shell with spinach mixture. Place shells in casserole.

8. Cook onion in skillet with reserved drippings until tender but not brown.

9. Add tomatoes and tomato sauce. Bring to a boil.

10. Pour over shells.

11. Sprinkle with remaining bacon.

12. Cover and bake for 40 minutes.

Unbelievable Salad

INGREDIENTS:

- 1 can (15½ ounces) crushed pineapple
- 1 package (3 ounces) cherry-flavored gelatin
- 1 can (11 ounces) mandarin oranges, drained
- 1 carton (8 ounces) creamed cottage cheese
- 1 carton (4½ ounces) frozen whipped topping, thawed
- Lettuce leaves

EQUIPMENT:

Small saucepan
Large glass mixing bowl
Wooden spoon
8-inch square dish

1. Pour the pineapple with its juice into a small saucepan. Cook over medium heat until juice comes to a boil, about 4 to 6 minutes. Remove from heat. Pour gelatin mix into large glass mixing bowl. Carefully pour pineapple and juice into bowl.

2. Stir with a wooden spoon until gelatin is dissolved. Chill in the refrigerator until it is cool and begins to thicken, about 2 hours.

3. Remove from refrigerator and stir in the oranges, cottage cheese, and whipped topping. Pour into the square dish. Refrigerate until firm.

4. Cut into squares and serve on lettuce leaves.

Layered Tomato Salad

INGREDIENTS:

- 4 large tomatoes
- 1 cup fresh parsley
  Fresh basil, chopped, *or* dried basil
- ¾ cup Italian salad dressing

EQUIPMENT:

Measuring cups
Sharp knife
Kitchen scissors
1-quart serving bowl
Plastic wrap

1. Cut core out of tomatoes and slice tomatoes thinly using knife.

2. Snip parsley into small pieces using scissors.

3. Place 1 layer of tomatoes in bottom of bowl. Sprinkle with some basil and parsley.

4. Continue layering tomatoes, basil, and parsley.

5. Pour dressing over top.

6. Cover with plastic wrap. Chill 2 to 3 hours before serving.

Easy Waldorf Salad

Makes 4 servings

INGREDIENTS:

  3 cups diced, unpeeled red apples
  1 cup diced celery
  ½ cup mayonnaise
    Lettuce
  ½ cup walnut pieces
    Cinnamon

EQUIPMENT:

  Measuring cups
  Knife
  Bowl

1. Dice apples and celery with knife.

2. Combine apples, celery, and mayonnaise in bowl. Mix.

3. Serve on lettuce leaves; sprinkle with walnuts and cinnamon.

Marinated Bean Salad

Makes 8 to 10 servings

INGREDIENTS:

  1 can (16 ounces) cut green beans, drained
  1 can (16 ounces) yellow wax beans, drained
  1 can (15 ounces) kidney beans, drained
  1 can (8½ ounces) green lima beans, drained
  ½ cup chopped green pepper
  ½ cup sugar
  ½ cup vinegar
  ⅓ cup salad oil
  1 tablespoon dry minced onion
  1 teaspoon seasoned salt
  1 teaspoon celery seed
  ¼ teaspoon pepper

EQUIPMENT:

  2-quart glass bowl
  Measuring cups and spoons
  Small saucepan
  Teaspoon
  Wooden spoon

1. In a glass bowl, combine the green beans, wax beans, kidney beans, lima beans, and green pepper. Set aside.

2. In a small saucepan, combine the sugar, vinegar, oil, onion, seasoned salt, celery seed, and pepper. Cook on medium for about 5 minutes, just until boiling.

3. Carefully remove from heat. Stir with a teaspoon to combine all the ingredients.

4. Pour hot dressing over the beans. Stir with a wooden spoon.

5. Salad can be served immediately, or refrigerate for several hours and serve chilled.

10-Layer Salad

Makes 6 to 8 servings

INGREDIENTS:

1 cup mayonnaise
¼ cup dairy sour cream
1 teaspoon instant minced onion
½ teaspoon salt
1 head lettuce, washed
1 10-ounce package frozen baby peas, thawed
1 2-ounce bottle green olives
1 8-ounce package mozzarella *or* Cheddar cheese, shredded

EQUIPMENT:

Measuring cups and spoons
Small mixing bowl
Mixing spoon
2-quart salad bowl
Kitchen scissors
Plastic wrap

1. Mix mayonnaise, sour cream, onion, and salt in mixing bowl using mixing spoon. Set aside.

2. Tear lettuce into bite-size pieces using fingers.

3. Spread half of lettuce in salad bowl. Top with half of peas.

4. Cut olives into small pieces with scissors. Spread half over peas.

5. Spoon half of mayonnaise mixture over olives. Sprinkle half of cheese over mayonnaise.

6. Repeat layers 1 more time, beginning with lettuce and ending with cheese.

7. Cover with plastic wrap. Refrigerate until serving time.

Crunchy Salad Delight

Makes 4 to 5 servings

INGREDIENTS:

1 small head cabbage
1 medium red apple
1 cup miniature marshmallows
1 teaspoon lemon juice
½ cup pineapple yogurt
2 tablespoons chopped nuts

EQUIPMENT:

Cutting board
Sharp knife
Medium-sized bowl
Fork

1. Chop cabbage into small pieces until you have enough to measure 2 cups. Place in bowl.

2. Wash apple and chop into ¼-inch pieces. Add to bowl. Add marshmallows, lemon juice, and yogurt; toss with fork.

3. Sprinkle with chopped nuts just before serving.

Summer Salad

Makes 6 servings

INGREDIENTS:

- 1 8-ounce can green beans, drained
- 1 8-ounce can sliced carrots, drained
- 1 8-ounce can sliced potatoes, drained
- 1 large tomato
- 1 cup Italian salad dressing
- 1 tablespoon instant minced onion
- ¼ teaspoon garlic powder
- ½ cup mayonnaise

EQUIPMENT:

Measuring cups and spoons
Large mixing bowl
Mixing spoon
Sharp knife
Plastic wrap

1. Combine vegetables in mixing bowl using mixing spoon.

2. Take core out of tomato and chop tomato into small pieces using sharp knife.

3. Add to bowl with dressing, onion, and garlic powder. Stir.

4. Cover with plastic wrap. Refrigerate overnight.

5. Drain dressing from vegetables when ready to serve.

6. Stir in mayonnaise. Serve immediately.

Note: Green peppers make handy serving "bowls." Cut off stem end and scoop out seeds and any white membrane. Spoon salad into peppers. Place on serving platter and surround with lettuce to garnish.

Cream Cheese Shamrocks

Makes 6 servings

INGREDIENTS:

- 6 lettuce leaves
- 1 large green pepper
- 2 stalks celery
- 6 radishes
- 2 3-ounce packages cream cheese with chives, softened
- Finely chopped parsley *or* chives to garnish

EQUIPMENT:

6 salad plates
Sharp knife
Small mixing bowl
Mixing spoon

1. Place lettuce leaf on each of 6 salad plates.

2. Slice off stem end of pepper with sharp knife. Cut into 6 ¼-inch rings. Remove seeds.

3. Place ring on lettuce.

4. Chop celery and radishes into small pieces.

5. Mix cream cheese, celery, and radishes in mixing bowl using mixing spoon.

6. Divide mixture among rings, mounding cheese in center.

7. Sprinkle with parsley or chives, if desired.

Cream Cheese Shamrocks, Summer Salad, this page; Layered Tomato Salad, 27; Chick and Chips, 47

INVITING VEGETABLES

Smart Snacks with Wonder Dip

Makes 3 to 4 servings

INGREDIENTS:

Assorted fresh vegetables
  Select 3 or 4 of your
  favorites from this list:
    Cauliflower florets
    Green pepper rings
    Cherry tomatoes
    Carrot sticks
    Celery sticks
    Raw mushrooms
    Broccoli florets
Lettuce leaves, washed and
  dried
Wonder Dip (recipe follows)

EQUIPMENT:

Large plate *or* platter

1. Ask an adult to help you with cleaning and cutting the assorted vegetables into bite-size pieces.

2. Line a large plate with lettuce leaves.

3. Arrange the vegetables over the lettuce in a pretty design. Leave a space in the middle for a small bowl of Wonder Dip.

Wonder Dip

Makes 1½ cups

INGREDIENTS:

  1 cup sour cream
  ½ cup plain yogurt
  1 package (½ ounce)
    green onion dip mix

EQUIPMENT:

  Small mixing bowl
  Rubber spatula
  Small serving bowl

1. Combine sour cream and yogurt in a small mixing bowl.

2. Blend in the dip mix with a rubber spatula.

3. Spoon into small serving bowl and place on a vegetable platter.

Serving Tip: Wash a large green pepper. Remove the stem end with a small sharp knife. Discard the seeds. Serve the dip in the green pepper "bowl."

Corn on the Cob

Makes 4 servings

INGREDIENTS:

4 ears frozen corn on the
   cob
   Butter
   Salt and pepper

EQUIPMENT:

Large microwave-safe plate
Plastic wrap
Small paring knife
Potholders

1. Arrange corn on the plate, like the spokes of a wheel.

2. Cover with plastic wrap. (You will need to use two strips to cover it completely.) Tuck the ends of the plastic wrap under the plate. Use a small sharp knife to make 3 or 4 slits in the plastic wrap.

3. Microwave on HIGH for 6 minutes; rotate the plate a half-turn.

4. Microwave on HIGH for 6 to 7 more minutes. Carefully remove from the microwave, using potholders. Let stand 3 minutes before serving.

5. Serve with butter, salt, and pepper.

Easy Baked Beans

Makes 8 servings

INGREDIENTS:

3 slices uncooked
   bacon
1 onion
2 16-ounce cans pork
   and beans
½ cup brown sugar
2 tablespoons catsup
1 teaspoon prepared
   mustard
3 tablespoons dark
   molasses
4 slices cooked bacon,
   crumbled, optional

EQUIPMENT:

Measuring cups and spoons
Knife
2-quart casserole dish
Large spoon

1. Preheat oven to 325°.

2. Carefully cut uncooked bacon into small pieces.

3. Next, dice the onion.

4. Place uncooked bacon, onion, beans, brown sugar, catsup, mustard, and molasses in casserole dish. Mix well with a large spoon.

5. Bake for 40 minutes.

6. Garnish with cooked bacon, if desired.

Sweet Potato Casserole

Makes 8 servings

INGREDIENTS:

8 sweet potatoes
¼ teaspoon nutmeg
½ teaspoon cinnamon
¼ teaspoon salt
4 tablespoons oil
⅓ cup sugar
⅓ cup dark brown sugar
14 large marshmallows
½ cup pecan halves

EQUIPMENT:

Knife
Measuring cups and spoons
Large saucepan
Fork
Spoon
Greased casserole dish
Potholders

1. Preheat oven to 350°.

2. Pare and cut up sweet potatoes with knife.

3. Place in saucepan and just cover with water. Boil for 30 minutes or until tender.

4. Drain potatoes and mash with a fork.

5. Add remaining ingredients, except marshmallows and pecans. Mix well.

6. Spoon mixture into greased casserole; cover with marshmallows and pecan halves.

7. Bake for 30 minutes.

Mushrooms and Corn

Makes 4 servings

INGREDIENTS:

1 10-ounce package frozen whole kernel corn
1 cup sliced fresh mushrooms
2 tablespoons butter *or* margarine
1 tablespoon snipped parsley

EQUIPMENT:

Measuring cups and spoons
Saucepan
Skillet
Spoon

1. Cook corn in saucepan and drain.

2. Melt butter in skillet over low heat.

3. Cook and stir mushrooms over medium-high heat for 3 to 4 minutes or until tender.

4. Stir in corn and parsley and serve.

Corn on the Cob, 33;
Broccoli-Gee Whiz!, 36

Broccoli–Gee Whiz!

Makes 4 servings

INGREDIENTS:

1 package (10 ounces)
   frozen broccoli spears
   Cheese Sauce (recipe
   follows)

EQUIPMENT:

1-quart microwave-safe
   casserole with cover
Potholders, optional

1. Place broccoli in a covered casserole. Microwave on HIGH for 4 minutes; rotate a half-turn.

2. Microwave on HIGH for 2 minutes more; carefully remove from microwave.

3. Let broccoli stand covered for 5 minutes before serving. Make Cheese Sauce and pour over cooked broccoli spears.

Cheese Sauce

Makes 1 cup

INGREDIENTS:

1 cup milk
2 tablespoons cornstarch
¼ teaspoon salt
1 tablespoon butter
1 cup (4 ounces) shredded
   American cheese *or*
   Cheddar cheese

EQUIPMENT:

2-cup glass measure
Measuring spoons and cups
Small whisk
Rubber spatula

1. Pour milk into glass measure. Add cornstarch and salt; whisk to combine and to dissolve any lumps. Add the butter.

2. Microwave on HIGH 1½ minutes; whisk well.

3. Microwave on HIGH for 30 seconds. The sauce will start to thicken near the edges. Whisk well.

4. Microwave on HIGH for 20 to 35 seconds, just until thickened.

5. Carefully remove from the microwave. With a rubber spatula, stir in the cheese. Let stand 1 or 2 minutes. Stir again to blend.

6. Serve Cheese Sauce over cooked broccoli spears or other cooked vegetables.

Potaddies

Makes 6 servings

INGREDIENTS:

4 baking potatoes
2 tablespoons vegetable oil
¼ cup butter *or* margarine, softened
Salt and ground black pepper

EQUIPMENT:

Sharp knife
Measuring spoons
10 x 15-inch baking pan
Table knife
Metal spatula

1. Preheat oven to 400°.

2. Cut potatoes lengthwise into ½-inch slices using sharp knife.

3. Drizzle oil over bottom of pan.

4. Spread 1 teaspoon of butter with table knife on one side of each potato slice as if buttering bread.

5. Place potato slices, buttered-side-up, in pan.

6. Bake 25 to 30 minutes or until light brown and slightly crisp.

7. Sprinkle with salt and pepper. Remove from pan using spatula. Serve immediately.

Buttered Carrots and Onions

Makes 4 servings

INGREDIENTS:

8 medium carrots
1 small onion
2 tablespoons butter *or* margarine
¼ teaspoon salt

EQUIPMENT:

Vegetable parer
Cutting board
Sharp knife
Large skillet with cover
Fork
Slotted spoon

1. Wash and pare carrots. Cut lengthwise into quarters on cutting board, then cut again into 2-inch sticks. Peel onions; slice into ⅛-inch-thick rings.

2. Melt butter in skillet; add carrots and onions. Add enough water to just cover carrots. Sprinkle with salt.

3. Cover and cook over medium heat for 15 to 20 minutes or until carrots are tender when pierced with a fork.

4. Remove from pan with a slotted spoon. Gently stir in additional butter, if desired.

DELICIOUS DESSERTS

Baked Apples

INGREDIENTS:

  6 apples
  ½ cup packed brown sugar
  ½ teaspoon ground
      cinnamon
  1 cup water

EQUIPMENT:

  Apple corer
  Knife
  Covered baking dish
  Bowl
  Measuring cups and spoons
  Spoon
  Potholder
  Fork

1. Preheat oven to 350°.
2. Wash and dry apples.
3. Remove cores with corer.
4. Peel off a strip of skin around top of each hole made by the corer.
5. Put apples in baking dish.
6. Combine brown sugar and cinnamon.
7. Fill apples with mixture.
8. Pour water around apples.
9. Put cover on baking dish and bake for one hour.
10. Prick with fork to test for doneness. Apples should be easy to prick.

Very Berry Pie

INGREDIENTS:

  1 3¼-ounce package vanilla pudding mix
  1 8-ounce package cream cheese, softened
  ½ teaspoon vanilla
  1 8-inch graham cracker piecrust
  20 to 25 strawberries, hulled
  1 pint blueberries
    Whipped cream *or* topping, optional

EQUIPMENT:

  Measuring spoons
  Medium-sized saucepan
  Rotary beater
  Mixing spoon

1. Prepare pudding mix in saucepan according to package directions.
2. Remove from heat and add cream cheese. Beat with rotary beater until smooth.
3. Stir in vanilla using mixing spoon.
4. Pour into crust.
5. Refrigerate 3 hours or overnight.
6. Place strawberries in circle around outer edge of pie and put 1 large strawberry in center of pie just before serving. Place blueberries to fill in remaining area.
7. Serve with whipped cream, if desired.

Zebra Parfaits

Makes 4 servings

INGREDIENTS:

  1 box (3½ ounces) instant chocolate pudding mix
  2 cups milk
  1 carton (4 ounces) refrigerated whipped topping
  4 stemmed maraschino cherries, optional

EQUIPMENT:

  Measuring cup
  Large mixing bowl
  Mixer
  Wooden spoon
  4 parfait glasses
  Spoon

1. Prepare the chocolate pudding with 2 cups milk, following package directions.

2. When the pudding is prepared, layer it with the whipped topping in parfait glasses. Start with chocolate pudding and finish with whipped topping. There should be about three layers of each.

3. Top each serving with a cherry.

Fruit Pops

Makes 1½ to 2 dozen

INGREDIENTS:

  1 3-ounce package gelatin (any flavor)
  1 envelope instant unsweetened soft drink mix
  1 cup sugar
  2 cups boiling water
  2 cups cold water

EQUIPMENT:

  Large bowl
  Spoon
  Soup *or* punch ladle
  Measuring cups
  Ice cube trays *or* paper cups
  Wooden sticks *or* ice cream spoons

1. Mix gelatin, instant soft drink mix, and sugar with boiling water in large bowl. Stir until dissolved.

2. Add cold water.

3. Ladle into ice cube trays or paper cups.

4. Insert wooden sticks or spoons diagonally in each section or cup. (Pops may be partially frozen before inserting sticks.)

5. Freeze until firm (2 or 3 hours).

Brownie-Mint Cookies

Makes 2½ to 3 dozen

INGREDIENTS:

- 1 **cup granulated sugar**
- ½ **cup butter** *or* **margarine, softened**
- 2 **eggs**
- 2 **squares unsweetened chocolate, melted**
- 1 **teaspoon baking powder**
- 1 **cup flour**
- ¼ **teaspoon salt**
- 1 **teaspoon vanilla**
- ½ **cup chopped nuts**
- ½ **cup crushed peppermint candies**

EQUIPMENT:

Measuring cups and spoons
Baking sheet
Mixing spoon
Large mixing bowl
Spoon
Metal spatula
Wire rack

1. Preheat oven to 350°. Grease baking sheet.

2. Stir sugar, butter, and eggs with mixing spoon in mixing bowl.

3. Stir in chocolate.

4. Blend in all remaining ingredients.

5. Drop dough by teaspoons 2 inches apart on baking sheet.

6. Bake 8 to 9 minutes. Don't overbake.

7. Using spatula, place cookies on rack to cool. Store in airtight container.

Banana Freeze

Makes 1 serving

INGREDIENTS:

- ½ **banana, cut into pieces and frozen**
- ¼ **cup evaporated milk, chilled**
- ½ **teaspoon vanilla extract**
- 2 **teaspoons sugar**
  Ice cubes, optional

EQUIPMENT:

Measuring cups and spoons
Blender
Tall glass

1. In blender, combine all ingredients.

2. Blend until mixture is smooth and thickened.

3. Add ice cubes to thicken even more.

4. Serve in tall glass.

Strawberry Shortcakes

Makes 4 servings

INGREDIENTS:

    4 individual dessert
        sponge cakes
    1 pint vanilla ice cream
        Strawberry Sauce
        (recipe below)
        Sliced almonds, optional

EQUIPMENT:

    4 dessert plates
    Ice cream scoop
    Tablespoon

1. Place a sponge cake on each dessert plate.

2. Top each with a generous scoop of vanilla ice cream.

3. Top with 2 or 3 tablespoons of Strawberry Sauce. Serve immediately. Decorate with almonds if you like.

Strawberry Sauce

Makes about 2 cups

INGREDIENTS:

    1 package (16 ounces)
        frozen sliced
        strawberries
    ¼ cup sugar
    2 tablespoons cornstarch
    ¼ cup strawberry jam

EQUIPMENT:

    Medium-sized saucepan
    Wooden spoon
    Measuring cups and spoon
    Small mixing bowl

1. Empty strawberries into a medium-sized saucepan.

2. Cook over medium-low heat 10 to 15 minutes, or until berries are thawed and can be broken apart. Stir occasionally with a wooden spoon.

3. In a small bowl, combine the sugar and the cornstarch; mix well.

4. Pour the mixture into the pan with the berries; stir with wooden spoon.

5. Continue cooking over medium-low heat until mixture comes to a boil, about 5 to 10 minutes.

6. Remove pan from heat. Add jam. Let stand 1 minute, then mix.

7. Serve warm over ice cream or cake. Refrigerate leftover sauce in a covered container and use within a few days.

Apple-Blueberry Crisp

Makes 6 servings

INGREDIENTS:

  1 21-ounce can apple pie
     filling
  1 cup fresh *or* frozen
     blueberries
  1 teaspoon lemon juice
  ¼ cup quick-cooking rolled
     oats
  ¼ cup flour
  ¼ cup brown sugar
  ½ teaspoon cinnamon
  ¼ cup butter *or* margarine
     Vanilla ice cream,
     optional

EQUIPMENT:

Large bowl
9-inch pie plate
Small bowl
Pastry blender *or* 2 knives

1. Preheat oven to 350°.
2. Combine pie filling, blueberries, and lemon juice in large bowl. Mix well.
3. Turn into 9-inch pie plate.
4. In small bowl, combine oats, flour, brown sugar, and cinnamon.
5. Cut in butter with pastry blender until mixture resembles coarse crumbs.
6. Sprinkle over fruit.
7. Bake for 25 to 30 minutes or until bubbly.
8. Serve warm and top with ice cream, if desired.

Chocolate Soda

Makes 1 serving

INGREDIENTS:

  ¼ cup chilled club soda
  3 tablespoons chocolate
     syrup
  2 scoops vanilla ice cream
     Additional club soda
     Whipped topping
     Maraschino cherry

EQUIPMENT:

Measuring cups and spoons
Tall glass
Ice cream scoop

1. Combine club soda and chocolate syrup in tall glass.
2. Carefully add ice cream.
3. Fill glass with extra club soda.
4. Top with whipped topping and maraschino cherry.
5. Serve immediately.

Cherry Crisp Cups

Makes 5 servings

INGREDIENTS:

- 1 can (21 ounces) cherry pie filling
- ½ cup firmly packed brown sugar
- ⅓ cup flour
- ⅓ cup oats
- 3 tablespoons butter
  Whipped cream, optional

EQUIPMENT:

- 5 custard cups
- Measuring cups
- Small mixing bowl
- Fork
- 1-cup glass measure
- Potholders, optional

1. Spoon pie filling evenly into 5 custard cups.

2. Combine brown sugar, flour, and oats in a small mixing bowl. Stir with a fork until blended.

3. Place butter in a glass measure. Microwave on HIGH for 20 to 30 seconds, until melted; pour into flour mixture. Toss with a fork until mixed.

4. Sprinkle evenly over the cherry pie filling.

5. Place the custard cups in a circle inside the microwave. Microwave on HIGH for 3½ minutes.

6. Give the cups a quarter-turn.

7. Microwave on HIGH for 2 to 3 minutes, until the tops are toasty and the cherry mixture bubbles.

8. Carefully remove from the microwave, using potholders, if necessary. Let cool for several minutes.

9. Serve warm or cold and decorate with whipped cream, if desired.

Jiffy S'mores

Makes 1 serving

INGREDIENTS:

- 2 graham cracker squares
- 1 tablespoon peanut butter
- 1 tablespoon marshmallow cream
- ½ chocolate bar

EQUIPMENT:

- Measuring spoon
- Knife

1. Spread peanut butter on one graham cracker square.

2. Top with chocolate.

3. Spread marshmallow cream on remaining graham cracker square and place marshmallow-side down on the chocolate.

PARTY & HOLIDAY PIZAZZ

Cheese Twists

Makes 6 to 8 servings

INGREDIENTS:

- 1 17¼-ounce package frozen puff pastry sheets
- ½ cup butter *or* margarine
- ½ cup grated Parmesan cheese
- 2 tablespoons poppy seeds

EQUIPMENT:

Measuring cups and spoons
Small saucepan
Pastry brush
10 x 15-inch baking sheet
Table knife
Metal spatula
Wire rack

1. Thaw puff pastry sheets in package for 30 minutes.
2. Preheat oven to 425°.
3. Melt butter in saucepan over low heat.
4. Place pastry sheets on counter.
5. Brush with melted butter, using pastry brush.
6. Sprinkle with cheese and poppy seeds.
7. Cut each lengthwise into 2 rectangles, using table knife.
8. Cut each rectangle crosswise into ½-inch strips.
9. Twist strips and place on baking sheet. Bake 10 to 12 minutes.
10. Use spatula to remove twists from baking sheet. Place on wire rack to cool.

Chick & Chips

Makes 6 servings

INGREDIENTS:

- ½ cup evaporated milk
- ½ teaspoon poultry seasoning
- 3 cups finely crushed potato chips
- 10 to 12 chicken legs

EQUIPMENT:

Measuring cups and spoons
8 x 10-inch baking dish
2 deep plates *or* shallow bowls

1. Preheat oven to 375°. Generously grease dish.
2. Mix evaporated milk and poultry seasoning in deep plate.
3. Spread crushed chips on another deep plate.
4. Dip each chicken piece first in milk mixture and then in chips.
5. Place in baking dish.
6. Bake 40 to 50 minutes or until meat is tender.

Party Cheese Ball

Serves 20

INGREDIENTS:

- 1 8-ounce package cream cheese, softened
- 2 cups (8 ounces) crumbled blue cheese
- 1/3 cup flaked coconut
- 1 teaspoon finely grated onion
- 1 teaspoon Worcestershire sauce
- 1/4 cup coconut
- 1/4 cup chopped pecans
- 1/4 cup minced parsley
- 1 box crackers

EQUIPMENT:

Electric Mixer
Spoon
Measuring cups and spoons
Wax paper
Serving platter

1. Combine cheeses in mixing bowl and cream together with mixer.

2. Blend in the 1/3 cup coconut, onion, and Worcestershire sauce.

3. Cover and chill at least 6 hours.

4. Before serving, combine the 1/4 cup coconut, pecans, and parsley, and put on a piece of wax paper.

5. Form a ball with the cheese mixture and roll in coconut, pecan, parsley mixture until completely covered.

6. Place on platter and serve with crackers.

Party Platter Crunch

Makes 4 servings

INGREDIENTS:

- 1/2 cup butter or margarine
- 1 tablespoon soy sauce
- 1/4 teaspoon garlic salt
- 1/4 teaspoon onion salt
- 1 5-ounce can chow mein noodles or 5 ounces pretzel sticks
- 1 cup square rice cereal
- 1 cup peanuts

EQUIPMENT:

Measuring cups and spoons
Small saucepan
10 x 15-inch jelly roll pan
Wooden mixing spoon

1. Preheat oven to 275°.

2. Melt butter in saucepan.

3. Add soy sauce, garlic, and onion salts and stir with wooden mixing spoon.

4. Spread chow mein noodles, rice cereal, and peanuts on jelly roll pan.

5. Drizzle with butter mixture and stir to coat.

6. Bake 5 minutes; stir well and bake another 5 minutes until light brown.

7. Cool and store in airtight container.

Firecrackers

Makes 4 to 6 servings

INGREDIENTS:

1 6-ounce can frozen
 grape juice
 concentrate, thawed
4 cups lemon-lime soda
1 pint vanilla ice cream

EQUIPMENT:

Measuring cup
3-quart pitcher
Mixing spoon
4 to 6 glasses
Ice cream scoop

1. Pour concentrate into pitcher.

2. Stir in soda using mixing spoon.

3. Put 2 scoops ice cream into each glass using ice cream scoop.

4. Pour grape drink over ice cream.

5. Serve immediately with straw, if desired.

Mexican Munch Olé

Makes about 8 cups

INGREDIENTS:

½ cup butter
1 tablespoon taco
 seasoning mix
2 cups corn chips
2 cups crisp corn cereal
 squares
1 cup crisp rice cereal
 squares
1 cup peanuts
2 cups pretzel sticks

EQUIPMENT:

1-cup glass measure
Fork
Measuring cups and spoons
9 x 13-inch glass baking
 dish
Potholders

1. Put butter in a glass measure. Microwave on HIGH for 1 minute, or until butter is melted. Remove from microwave. Stir in the taco seasoning mix with a fork; set aside.

2. Combine the corn chips, cereals, pretzels, and peanuts in the baking dish.

3. Drizzle with the butter mixture; stir with a fork.

4. Microwave on HIGH for 2 minutes. Open the oven door and stir the mixture with a fork. Microwave on HIGH for another 1 to 2 minutes, until heated through.

5. With potholders, remove from the oven. Cool before serving.

6. Store any leftover Mexican Munch in a sealed glass jar or plastic bag.

Stained Glass Window Cookies   Makes 2½ to 3 dozen

INGREDIENTS:

- ½ cup dark corn syrup
- ½ cup granulated sugar
- ½ cup butter
- ½ cup milk
- ½ teaspoon ground ginger
- 1 teaspoon ground cinnamon
- ½ teaspoon baking soda
- 3½ to 3¾ cups all-purpose flour
- Assorted colored hard candies

EQUIPMENT:

Measuring cups and spoons
Mixing spoon
Large mixing bowl
Aluminum foil
10 x 15-inch baking sheet
Wire rack

1. Stir all ingredients except candy with mixing spoon in mixing bowl until smooth.

2. Chill 1 to 2 hours.

3. Preheat oven to 350°.

4. Crush each hard candy separately.

5. Place sheet of aluminum foil on baking sheet. Grease foil.

6. Roll each 1 to 2 tablespoons dough into pencil shape.

7. Form pencil shapes of dough 2 inches apart on foil into heart, church window, or flower shapes, leaving centers empty.

8. Fill empty spaces with crushed candy.

9. Bake 8 to 9 minutes. Cool cookies on foil 3 to 4 minutes.

10. Peel away foil and place cookies on rack to cool completely. Store in airtight tin.

Holiday Fancies   Makes 4 dozen

INGREDIENTS:

- 1½ cups pitted prunes
- 1 cup flaked coconut
- 1 cup chopped walnuts
- ⅔ cup sweetened condensed milk
- 1 cup chocolate jimmies

EQUIPMENT:

Measuring cups
Kitchen scissors
Mixing spoon
Large mixing bowl

1. Snip prunes into tiny pieces with kitchen scissors.

2. Stir prunes, coconut, and walnuts with mixing spoon in mixing bowl.

3. Stir in milk.

4. Shape mixture into 48 balls. Chill 30 minutes.

5. Roll in chocolate jimmies, lightly pressing jimmies into balls.

6. Store in airtight tin.

Stained Glass Window Cookies, Holiday Fancies, this page; Caramel-Pecan Crunchies, 55; Brownie-Mint Cookies, 41

Peanut Brittle Parfaits

Makes 4 servings

INGREDIENTS:

  1 3¾-ounce package
     instant butterscotch
     pudding mix
  2 cups milk
  ½ pound peanut brittle
     Whipped cream *or*
     topping

EQUIPMENT:

  Measuring cup
  Mixing bowl
  Rotary beater
  Plastic bag
  Rolling pin

1. Make pudding, according to package directions, in mixing bowl using rotary beater.

2. Put peanut brittle in plastic bag.

3. Gently hit with rolling pin to crush brittle.

4. Alternate layers of pudding and crushed peanut brittle in each of 4 dishes.

5. Sprinkle some crushed peanut brittle on top of each.

6. Top with dollop of whipped cream or topping. Serve immediately or refrigerate until serving time.

St. Pat's Parfaits

Makes 6 servings

INGREDIENTS:

 25 to 30 chocolate wafers
  1 cup sweetened
     condensed milk
  1 6-ounce can frozen
     limeade, thawed
  1 8-ounce container
     whipped topping *or* 1
     cup whipped cream
     Green food coloring
  2 tablespoons chocolate
     jimmies

EQUIPMENT:

  Measuring cups and spoons
  Blender
  Large mixing bowl
  Mixing spoon
  6 parfait glasses *or* bowls

1. Put wafers in blender. Process until crumbs form.

2. Pour milk and limeade into mixing bowl. Stir well with mixing spoon.

3. Stir in topping.

4. Add 1 or 2 drops food coloring and gently mix.

5. Place 2 or 3 spoonfuls of mixture in each parfait glass. Sprinkle with 1 tablespoon crumbs. Continue layering cream and crumbs, ending with cream.

6. Sprinkle 1 teaspoon jimmies on top of each parfait. Refrigerate until serving time.

Deviled Eggs in the Grass

Makes 1 dozen

INGREDIENTS:

 6 hard-boiled eggs, peeled
 2 tablespoons mayonnaise
 1 tablespoon mustard
 ¼ teaspoon salt
 3 olives, halved
 1 container (4 ounces)
   alfalfa sprouts

EQUIPMENT:

 1 styrofoam egg carton
 Paring knife
 Small cutting board
 Small mixing bowl
 Fork
 Measuring spoons
 Teaspoon

1. In hot soapy water, wash the styrofoam egg carton. Rinse in hot water and dry. Set aside.

2. Cut eggs in half horizontally on a cutting board. Gently remove the yolks and place them in a small mixing bowl; save the whites.

3. Mash the yolks with a fork. Add the mayonnaise, mustard, and salt; mix until smooth.

4. Using a teaspoon, carefully spoon the yolk mixture back into the whites. Top with olive halves.

5. Open the egg carton and arrange alfalfa sprouts in each of the egg holders, with the green portion up. Carefully place deviled eggs on the sprouts.

Note: These eggs are perfect to take on a picnic! Simply close the egg carton and they are ready to go!

Candy Easter Eggs

Makes 2 dozen

INGREDIENTS:

 1 3-ounce package cream
   cheese, softened
 2½ cups powdered sugar
 ½ teaspoon vanilla *or*
   almond *or* lemon *or*
   raspberry *or* coconut
   extract
 Food coloring, optional
 Assorted pastel-colored
   sugar crystals

EQUIPMENT:

 Measuring cups and spoons
 Large mixing bowl
 Mixing spoon
 Teaspoon
 Wax paper
 10 x 15-inch baking sheet

1. Mix cream cheese, powdered sugar, and extract in bowl with mixing spoon.

2. Stir in 1 or 2 drops of food coloring, if desired. Chill 30 minutes.

3. Form rounded teaspoons of mixture into egg shapes.

4. Roll in colored sugar.

5. Cover baking sheet with wax paper.

6. Place sugar-coated eggs on sheet.

7. Chill until set, 30 to 40 minutes. Store in refrigerator.

SATISFYING SNACKS

Hawaiian Ice

Makes about 5 servings

INGREDIENTS:

    Juice of 2 lemons
    Juice of 2 oranges
2   bananas, mashed
1   cup canned crushed
        pineapple and juice
¾   cup sugar
1   cup water
    Ginger ale
    Maraschino cherries *or*
        mint leaves, optional

EQUIPMENT:

Measuring cups
Bowl
Spoon
Ice cube trays

1. Combine all ingredients in bowl and blend well with a spoon.

2. Pour into ice cube trays and freeze.

3. When frozen, put 3 or 4 cubes in a glass and pour ginger ale over them.

4. Garnish with a maraschino cherry or mint leaves, if desired.

Caramel-Pecan Crunchies

Makes 5 dozen

INGREDIENTS:

20 marshmallows
20 vanilla caramel candies
2   tablespoons water
2   tablespoons butter
1   teaspoon vanilla
3   cups crisp rice cereal
½   cup chopped pecans

EQUIPMENT:

Measuring cups and spoons
9-inch square baking pan
Wooden mixing spoon
3-quart saucepan
Table knife

1. Grease pan.

2. Stir marshmallows, caramels, water, and butter with wooden mixing spoon in saucepan over low heat until caramels and marshmallows melt.

3. Remove from heat. Stir in vanilla.

4. Stir in cereal and nuts until well coated with caramel mixture.

5. Press into baking pan using mixing spoon.

6. Cool.

7. Cut into 1-inch squares using table knife dipped in hot water. Store in airtight tin.

Granola

Makes about 5½ cups

INGREDIENTS:

½ cup butter
½ cup honey
3 cups oats
¾ cup sunflower seeds
1 cup coarsely chopped
    peanuts
½ cup wheat germ
½ cup brown sugar
½ cup raisins

EQUIPMENT:

2-cup glass measure
Measuring cups
3-quart glass mixing bowl
Wooden spoon
Potholders
Cookie sheet
Covered container

1. Microwave butter on HIGH in glass measure for 30 to 40 seconds, until melted. Remove from the microwave; add the honey.

2. Place oats, sunflower seeds, peanuts, wheat germ, and brown sugar in a mixing bowl.

3. Add the melted butter and honey.

4. Mix well with a wooden spoon.

5. Microwave on HIGH for 4 minutes; stir.

6. Microwave on HIGH for 2 minutes; stir.

7. Microwave on HIGH for 1 minute. Add the raisins; stir.

8. Microwave on HIGH for 1 more minute, or until the mixture is toasty; stir.

9. With potholders, carefully remove from the microwave. Pour on a cookie sheet; spread with the back of a wooden spoon. When cool, store in a covered container.

Guacamole Dip with Vegetables

Makes 20 servings

INGREDIENTS:

2 ripe avocados
1 4-ounce container
    whipped cream cheese
Seasoned salt to taste
Carrots
Celery
Cauliflower
Broccoli

EQUIPMENT:

Knife
Spoon
Fork
Bowl
Serving dish

1. Cut avocados, remove seed, and scoop out insides with spoon.

2. Mash avocados in bowl with fork and mix with cream cheese and salt.

3. Place on one or two serving dishes with clean, sliced vegetables.

4. Refrigerate until serving time.

Crunch Munch Treats

Makes 2 dozen

INGREDIENTS:

- 1 tablespoon butter
- 1 package (14 ounces) caramels
- 3 tablespoons water
- 1 cup crisp corn cereal squares
- 1 cup bran cereal squares
- 1 cup crispy rice cereal
- 1 cup granola
- ½ cup shredded coconut
- 1½ cups salted peanuts
- ½ cup milk chocolate chips
- 1 tablespoon shortening

EQUIPMENT:

- 9 x 13-inch glass baking dish
- Paper towels
- 1-quart batter bowl
- Wooden spoon
- Measuring cups and spoons
- Large mixing bowl
- Tablespoon
- 1-cup glass measure

1. Lightly butter the baking dish. (To do this, put butter in the dish and push it around with a paper towel. It will leave a thin layer of butter on the bottom and keep the cookies from sticking.)

2. Remove caramel wrappings. Place the caramels in a batter bowl; add water. Microwave on HIGH for 1½ minutes; stir with a wooden spoon. Microwave on HIGH for another 1½ to 2 minutes, until caramels are melted.

3. Combine the cereals, granola, coconut, and peanuts in a large mixing bowl; toss together.

4. Carefully pour the caramel over the cereals. Stir gently until all the pieces are evenly coated. Pour into the buttered dish. Spread a little butter on the back of a tablespoon and gently press the mixture evenly into the dish.

5. Microwave the chocolate chips and shortening in a glass measure on HIGH for 1 minute; stir. Microwave on HIGH for 1 to 1½ minutes more, until chocolate is melted.

6. Very slowly drizzle the chocolate over the cereal mixture, making thin lines across the top.

7. Chill about 30 minutes or until chocolate is set.

8. Cut into squares.

Fish-n-Boats

Makes 2 servings

INGREDIENTS:

1 can (6 ounces) tuna, drained
½ cup mayonnaise
⅓ cup chopped celery
¼ cup sweet pickle relish, drained
2 large French rolls, about 6 inches long
½ cup shredded American cheese
1 slice American cheese
2 olives, sliced

EQUIPMENT:

Measuring cups and spoons
Small mixing bowl
Fork
Small cutting board
Small knife
10 x 15-inch baking sheet
Potholders
2 wooden skewers

1. Combine tuna, mayonnaise, celery, and pickle relish in mixing bowl. Stir well with a fork; set aside.

2. Place one French roll on a cutting board. Carefully cut a thin slice, lengthwise, off the top of the roll.

3. With your fingers, hollow out the roll by removing some of the soft bread; leave about a ½-inch shell. Prepare the other roll the same way.

4. Place the "boats" on a 10 x 15-inch baking sheet.

5. Sprinkle 2 tablespoons of shredded cheese into each "boat."

6. Fill the "boats" with tuna mixture. Sprinkle with remaining shredded cheese.

7. Place the baking sheet in oven under hot broiler for 1 to 2 minutes, or until cheese is melted. Carefully remove from oven.

8. Cut the slice of American cheese diagonally. Thread a wooden skewer through the cheese to make a sail. Place a sail in each "boat."

9. Top with sliced olives.

Nutty Haystacks

Makes 3 dozen

INGREDIENTS:

½ cup white sugar
½ cup white corn syrup
½ cup peanut butter
2 cups Chinese noodles
½ cup salted peanuts

EQUIPMENT:

1-quart batter bowl
Measuring cups
Wooden spoon
Teaspoon
Waxed paper, 18 inches long

1. Combine sugar and corn syrup in a small saucepan; stir with a wooden spoon. Cook over medium heat until the mixture comes to a full boil, about 5 minutes. Carefully remove from heat.

2. Stir the mixture with the wooden spoon. Add the peanut butter; stir until melted and completely blended.

3. Add the noodles and peanuts; stir until coated.

4. Use a teaspoon to drop the cookies on a sheet of greased waxed paper. They will become firm in 15 or 20 minutes.

Munchkin Meatballs

Makes 12 to 15 servings

INGREDIENTS:

¾ pound ground beef
1 egg
¼ cup bread crumbs
¼ teaspoon salt
  Dash pepper
½ cup water
⅓ cup dark brown sugar
¼ cup lemon juice
1 tablespoon catsup

EQUIPMENT:

Measuring cups and spoons
Large bowl
Saucepan with lid
Serving dish
Toothpicks

1. Combine ground beef, egg, bread crumbs, salt, and pepper in bowl. Mix well.

2. Form into small balls (approximately 30).

3. Combine water, brown sugar, lemon juice, and catsup in saucepan.

4. Heat to a boil, then add meatballs.

5. Cover and simmer on low heat for 15 minutes.

6. Serve in dish with toothpicks.

My Hero

Makes 1 generous serving

INGREDIENTS:

1 submarine roll, partially split
2 tablespoons mayonnaise
  Lettuce leaves
1 slice American and mozzarella cheese, cut in half diagonally
2 thin slices each roast beef, ham, and salami
4 dill pickle slices
3 black olives, sliced

EQUIPMENT:
Table knife
Plate

1. Place the split roll on a plate. Open it so it will lay flat; spread with mayonnaise.

2. Place lettuce on roll.

3. Place the American cheese halves on lettuce with points extending outward.

4. Roll up the beef slices and place on the cheese. Do the same with the ham and salami.

5. Top with mozzarella cheese.

6. Garnish with pickle slices and olives.

Pizza Planks

Makes 6 servings

INGREDIENTS:

- 1 loaf (12 inches) French bread
- 1 jar (12 ounces) spaghetti sauce
- 1 package (4 ounces) sliced pepperoni
- 1 jar (2½ ounces) sliced mushrooms, drained
- 12 ounces shredded mozzarella cheese
- 2 tablespoons grated Parmesan cheese

EQUIPMENT:

Cutting board
Serrated knife
10 x 15-inch baking sheet
Measuring spoons

1. Preheat oven to 400°.

2. Ask an adult to assist you in splitting the loaf of bread. Place the bread on a cutting board. Carefully split bread in half lengthwise. Remove some of the soft bread to make a slightly hollowed loaf.

3. Place each half on the baking sheet, cut-sides up. Spoon spaghetti sauce evenly over both halves. Arrange pepperoni, mushrooms, and mozzarella cheese evenly over the tops. Sprinkle with Parmesan cheese.

4. Bake for 10 to 15 minutes, until cheese is bubbly.

Note: Use your imagination when making Pizza Planks. Add your favorite ingredients—green peppers, onions, cooked sausage, and hot dogs are a few suggestions.

Egg Salad Sandwiches

Makes 6 sandwiches

INGREDIENTS:

- 6 eggs
- ½ cup finely chopped celery
- 1 tablespoon minced onion
- ⅓ cup mayonnaise
  Salt and pepper to taste
  Bread of your choice
  Lettuce, optional

EQUIPMENT:

Medium-sized saucepan
Sharp knife
Measuring cups and spoons
Long-handled spoon
Medium-sized mixing bowl
Mixing spoon

1. Place eggs in medium-sized pan. Add enough cold water to come one inch above the eggs.

2. Cook over high heat until water begins to boil. Reduce heat to low and cook for 20 minutes.

3. Remove pan from heat and put under cold running water for 5 to 10 minutes. Refrigerate eggs until well chilled.

4. Crack, peel, and chop eggs. Put the chopped egg in medium-sized mixing bowl. Add remaining ingredients and mix well.

5. Spread egg salad on your favorite bread and top with lettuce, if desired.

Pop-a-Pizza

Makes 4 servings

INGREDIENTS:

4 **English muffins, split**
4 **slices salami lunch meat**
1 **can (10½ ounces) pizza sauce**
8 **ounces mozzarella cheese, shredded**
  Chopped green peppers, optional
  Cooked sausage, optional
  Black olives, optional
  Parmesan cheese, optional

EQUIPMENT:

10 x 15-inch baking pan
Cutting board
Pizza cutter
Tablespoon
Potholders

1. Preheat oven to 400°. Place 4 English muffin halves on 10 x 15-inch baking pan.

2. Stack the salami slices on a small cutting board. Cut the salami into thin long strips, using a pizza cutter. Then cut each strip in half; set aside.

3. Spread 1 or 2 tablespoons pizza sauce over each muffin half.

4. Divide salami strips evenly over the muffin halves.

5. Sprinkle generously with mozzarella cheese.

6. Place in oven and bake for 8 to 10 minutes, or until the cheese is bubbly. Carefully remove from oven. Serve immediately.

7. Decorate with remaining ingredients, if desired.

Cheese Buds

Makes 20 servings

INGREDIENTS:

2 **cups flour**
½ **pound butter *or* margarine, softened**
½ **pound grated Cheddar cheese, room temperature**
  Salt and ground red pepper to taste
  Pecan halves

EQUIPMENT:

Measuring cups
Blender
Spatula
Cookie sheet

1. Preheat oven to 400°.

2. In mixer, blend flour, butter, cheese, and seasonings.

3. Pinch off small, half-dollar-sized pieces and place on cookie sheet.

4. Top with pecan halves.

5. Bake for 15 minutes.

6. Cool and eat.